JOB SATISFACTION OF TEACHERS

DR. SAVITA MISHRA

I hereby declare that the book entitled "**Job Satisfaction of Teachers**" written by me is my original research work and has not been published earlier. I also declare that no chapter of this manuscript in whole or in part is lifted and incorporated in this report from any earlier work done by others or me.

Dr. Savita Mishra

Contents

Preface

Teachers have always played vital roles in the reconstruction of the society. In the event of universalisation of elementary education, therefore much emphasis was placed on recruitment of teachers. Teachers are accorded great due to their manipulative skills in igniting the inherent talents of the children. Hence NCTE (1998) put emphasis on teacher education as only enlightened and emancipated teachers can lead communities and nations in there march towards better and higher quality of life. Recent thrust on elementary education is intended to increase enrolment, retention and reduce drop and rates by achieving success through SSA/DPEP programs. The successful running of any educational system depends mainly upon the teacher, the pupil, the curriculum, and the facilities. Of these, the teacher is the most important one and is the pivot on whom the entire educational structure rests.

In order to strengthen the educational system it is indispensable to bring quality in primary education. First because a strong and healthy primary education can help in building the entire educational ladder up to the fullest perfection. Therefore much importance is to given to the primary level. In this context the national policy of education (1986) in its programme of action (1992) has envisaged a strong knowledge based, work oriented primary education system through appropriate curricular, sufficient infrastructure provision of women teachers, supply of the teaching materials, through a scheme called operational black board.

Teachers with dedication, devotion and commitment are hence required to run the institution. Therefore, requirement of teachers at the elementary level has been given the topmost priority. In the present juncture teachers even with higher qualification prefer to work in elementary school. But the question remain whether they are satisfied with job of teaching in the elementary school eludes everybody. Teacher's accountability to the pupils, their parents, and community and to their own profession is a matter of grave concern in the present context. Hence, the importance of good teaching staff in the process of education is the only criterion to step in the progress of developing countries.

Dr. Savita Mishra

Acknowledgements

The investigator is highly grateful to **Dr. B. K. Jha** for his academic support, constant encouragement, immense inspiration and scholarly guidance to complete this work.

The investigator expresses her gratitude to the **Head of the Institutes** and **all teachers** where the research work has been conducted and friends who have stretched their helping hands in collecting information.

The investigator is also grateful to **all the members of Vidyasagar College of Education, Phansidewa, Darjeeling, West Bengal** who have a little contribution for the present work.

Dr. Savita Mishra

CHAPTER ONE

INTRODUCTION

Teachers have always played vital roles in the reconstruction of the society. In the event of universalisation of elementary education, therefore much emphasis was placed on recruitment of teachers. Teachers are accorded great due to their manipulative skills in igniting the inherent talents of the children. Hence NCTE (1998) put emphasis on teacher education as only enlightened and emancipated teachers can lead communities and nations in there march towards better and higher quality of life. Recent thrust on elementary education is intended to increase enrolment, retention and reduce drop and rates by achieving success through SSA/DPEP programs. Hence the following activities were given due importance.

- Operation Blackboard scheme.
- Strengthening of teacher education in content and pedagogy.
- Nutritional support for all children.
- Making the school an attractive place.
- Innovative and alternative education.
- Inclusive Education.

In all these activities, teacher improvement was the only solution. Hence capacity building of teachers thought to be the priority area at the primary level. Therefore a community based SSA was launched. Under SSA intervention, immediate recruitment of Para teachers was made who were directed to work as primary school teachers. They were given in service training and hints to look into the quality dimensions of education with a paltry salary not commensurate with their educational qualifications. But whether teachers working at that level are satisfied or not, this was where looked. Hence the target of reaching at the aim of universalisation of elementary education is skill at stake. This has been quite pertinent from the reviews cited here under. The successful running of any educational system depends mainly upon the teacher, the pupil, the curriculum, and the facilities. Of these, the teacher is the most important one and is the pivot on whom the entire educational structure rests. Teacher was regarded as a holy person in ancient India; he was compared to a God. He is to be treated as a combination of the Trinity (Brahma, Vishu, Maheswara) as well as the supreme one. Thus, teacher was regarded as the most perfect being in those days and teaching was considered as a holy duty. As per our Indian ancestors, the "Teacher" is God. Further, it is said, 'Guru Brahma, Guru Vishnu, Gurudeva Maheswara' which implies that the teacher is the creator, the sustainer and the ultimate liberator. Centuries ago, in this Indian Land of Vedas, certain principles which had something noble and uplifting about them were held steadfastly. These principles were emphasized in those famous verses in Sanskrit, which the teacher and the taught recited together an considered the essence of their mutual relationship: "Saha Naavavatoo/ Saha Naubhuraktu/Saha Viryam Karavahai/Tejarvi Naava Dhitamastu/ Mavidvisavahai": May he protect us both; May he save us both; May we do together great deeds; May our bearing be bright; May we have each other: Though the same lines are recited today, one does not always find the same zeal and the same enthusiasm. The teacher's image has unquestionably changed from an 'inner-directed' to that of a 'stereotype'.

The teacher was looked upon as 'Guru' or 'Acharya' and was given the top most portions in the professional hierarchy. The teacher had no need to worry his head over the mundane necessities of life in the olden days, and hence he was free to pursue his quest for knowledge. In those days, he was a perfect model for the students in every aspect of life. He was given full freedom in planning the curriculum, methods of instruction and evaluation. The student and so the society used to ''look up' at the 'Acharya' for guidance and not 'look down' upon him as it is being done today though along with other professions like medicine, law and engineering, teaching is also considered as a profession, may, it is said to be the noblest of all profession and in today's world of Science and technology dynamic forces are working with incredible speed bringing unexpected changes into the sphere of human life. Explosion of knowledge has been the latest cry of the developed and developing countries and probably nowhere do these rapid changes present greater problems than in the field of education. In the quality of a nation depends upon the quality of its education, so it is necessary to know which is most responsible for bringing quality in education. To this question, the most logical answer is the teacher. Teacher's ability and quality of teaching spark the challenge for learning by pupils. Education based on the most appropriate objectives and suitable organizational climate in the educational institutions may fail to be effective and largely wasted if the teachers are inefficient and inactive.

Teaching is a very complex activity and multidimensional in nature besides knowledge in theory, it demands on the part of the teachers a variety of skills and abilities to be displayed. As the skills and efficiency of the teacher largely influence the pupils learning, recruitment of efficient and skilled teacher into the educational system becomes an essential pre-requisite of improvement of the system. Therefore, it becomes primarily an obligation of education to obtain capable and efficient teachers as learning by pupils depends very much on upon the skill and potentiality of the teacher, how we exploits the potentialities of his pupils to acquire knowledge and skill. It has also been stressed in the National Policy of Education, 1986. In this connection in the Program of Action it has been categorically mentioned that there should be sincere attempt for a substantial improvement in the quality of teacher's education. Teacher's accountability to the pupils, their parents, and community and to their own profession is a matter of grave concern in the present context. Hence, the importance of good teaching staff in the process of education is the only criterion to step in the progress of developing countries.

1. Concept of Job Satisfaction:

Job satisfaction could be said that the felling of joy and pleasure that a person has at the work he is engaged is known as his job satisfaction. What does he feel about the work he does, decided it. It is linked with his set of mind. It seems to be his personal concern. This is not all. This could also be linked with the monetary rewards or the wages that he gets. As a whole all that, is there at his work place determines it What inspires him, gives him a sort of thrill to be his best at the job is a source of his job satisfaction. What keeps him out of place at the job, works against the job satisfaction that he could have. Job satisfaction serves him as his motivation to do the work. This influences his effectiveness at work. In this context, Chopra (1986) writes as: 'A basic tenet of personal work has long been that a satisfied employee, with a high morale is likely to get along better with other employees, will be more accepting of managements directives, will be more committed to achieving organizational goals and in general will be more productive this persists despite rather limited supportive research'.

The study of job satisfaction has its origin in the later part of the second decade of the twentieth century. It can perhaps be said to have begun with the famous Haio Thome studies conducted by Elton Mayo and his Harvard Colleagues in the Western Electric Company, Chicago in 1920 (Davis, 1977, 58). Job satisfaction implies the attitude of a person towards his job and profession. It expresses the amount of congruence between one's expectation of the job and the rewards that the job provides. Since job satisfaction involves expectations compared with rewards, it is related to equity and the psychological contract. The term job satisfaction is very often confused with other kinds of terms like attitudes and morale. Similarly, job satisfaction is not the same as moral, although it may contribute to morale. Morale is a group feeling and job satisfaction is an individual feelings. Moral is generated by the group and it is a byproduct of the group. Job satisfaction is indeed a complex, cumbersome and may sided concept. It is a general attitude which is the result of many specific attitudes in three areas, namely specific job factors, individual characteristics and group relationship outside the job. Davis (1977) observes that "job satisfaction is the favorableness or unfavouralenes with which employees views their work. It results when there is a fit between job characteristics and the wants of employees. It expresses the amount of congruence's between one's expectations of the job and the rewards that the job provides ". From the above definitions it can be concluded that job satisfaction is governed, to a large extent, by perceptions and expectations. Men work to satisfy their needs and they aspire and expect their work life to fulfill these needs. For perfect job satisfaction there should exist a one to one relationship between the perception of how well the job life fulfils the various needs and expectations or aspirations of the individual and the extent to which these needs are actually fulfilled. Any discrepancy between aspirations and perceptions account for dissatisfaction. Thus, the perceived or imagined judgment of how well the job life is satisfying the various needs, accounts for the degree of job satisfaction and dissatisfaction.

Job satisfaction is the result of varies attitudes possessed by an employee. In a narrow sense, their attitudes are related to the job and are concerned with such specific factors or wages, supervision, steadiness of employment, conditions of work, opportunities for advancement, recognition of ability, fair evaluation of work, social relations on the job, prompt settlement of grievances, fair treatment by employer, and other similar factors. However, other aspects such as employee's age, health, temperament, and level of aspiration should be considered. Again, his family relationships, social status and activities in organizations, like labor, political or social, contribute ultimately to job satisfaction. Job satisfaction or dissatisfaction is the result of various attitudes the person holds towards his job, towards related factors and towards life in general.

1. Factors of Job Satisfaction:

For keeping the right man on the right job, counselors must be alert to factors responsible for job satisfaction in working out predictable job choices with their pupils. Comparison studies show that a larger percentage of men than women are dissatisfied; that there is more dissatisfaction in large companies than in small companies; that skilled workers are more satisfied than semi-skilled workers; that a larger percentage of professional than managerial workers and a larger percentage of managerial than commercial workers are satisfied; that workers who had received school guidance shaved greater job satisfaction than those unguided, and that those, whose jobs are related to a vocational interest pattern, are more satisfied than other whose jobs are in the field other than that of their interest. Job satisfaction studies such as the ones reported by Robinson and Hoppach indicate that personal relations are more significant than company policies. Those who have their jobs, are usually less critical of superiors than are those who do not workers who produce less are more satisfied with their jobs. It is believed that total job satisfaction of an individual in terms of total by adjustment also contributes to job satisfaction. Every person is interested, at least to some degree, in monetary returns. He must earn enough to maintain himself and usually a family, even if he is willing to accept a low standard of living. Many people are willing to engage in any work that is not actually frustrating; they do not seek intrinsic satisfaction. If a job is tolerable, their primary concern is with the salary or wages and the general conditions under which they work. With respect to the conditions of work, most people can probably adjust to a rather wide range on the other hand for many; environment is important and may lead to either satisfaction or frustration. They compromise by accepting lower returns in order to work in a satisfactory environment.

Numerous studies show that workers become dissatisfied with their jobs or their job moral drops because of:

- Lack of Chances of advancement;
- Lack of feeling of security for the future;
- Poor physical conditions;
- Lack of chances to show initiative, redress grievances, get proper training for their job, develop group adjustment or participate in management;
- Promise made at the time of recruitment for high salary, position or title etc, are not fulfilled.

For the satisfaction in job, the opposite of these conditions exists. In addition, the worker knows that he has a number of advantages:

- Protection by insurance, pension, gratuity;
- Job has status in the eyes of his fellow workers, family or his social groups;
- Worker has a sense of achievement which is recognized;
- Worker is treated with respect by his superiors.

Studies of job satisfaction have revealed the following:

- Any job is more interesting and satisfying to an individual if he understands the importance of it and knows the relation his particular assignment holds with the entire pattern of the project.
- The degree of satisfaction from a particular job depends on the number of potentialities that it can draw and, low level jobs like assembly line or lower clerical jobs tend to become interesting and less satisfying to the persons occupying them.
- In order to be really satisfying, the job needs to give some kind of spiritual realization to the worker.

3. Dimensions of Teacher Job Satisfaction:

Of many dimensions, the researcher considered the following dimensions for measuring Teacher Job Satisfaction. They are:

- Professional
- Teaching Learning
- Innovation and
- Inter-personal relations.

i. **Professional** related to job security and social prestige, molding the young minds, getting appreciation from others, reaching problems of the students.

ii. **Teaching Learning** refer to problems of the students, new situations, successfully managing the classes, students active participation in the classes, innovative technique in teaching, systematic plan of the work.

iii. **Innovation** relates to creativity, innovative technique in teaching, participation of cultural activities, co-curricular and social welfare activities.

iv. **Inter-personal relations** refer to relations with colleagues, parents, students, higher authorities or any personnel confined to college.

Sarva Shiksha Abhiyan (SSA): SSA is a programme for universalisation of Elementary Education covering the entire country. It was started in 2001. The programme aims to provide useful & relevant free & compulsory elementary Education for all children in the age group 6 to 14 yr under RTE Act. 2009. It is an initiative to universalize and improve quality of education The programme has time bound objectives on one hand SSA is a programme with its own targets, norms & process, on the other hand it is an umbrella programme covering other programmes like DPEP, Lok Jumbish & the operational black board etc.SSA adopts, 'The Bottom-Up' process of planning, where in the felt needs of the served communities and educational needs of learners are well taken care of and the plan fits into the broad frame work of the 'SSA. SSA has emphasized the involvement of local people and stake holders in planning in view of the fact that the desired improvement & sustenance of the improved efficiency level cannot be achieved without the active involvement of the community in the schooling system. India has made long strides in the last 50 yrs. in the field of education. A know of programmes/schemes were launched during the last four decades for universalization of the Elementary Education. Some of those efforts have been in the field of primary education & a few also covering upper primary sector. However, much needs to be done for the special focus groups & the upper primary sector. '

Strategies and Intervention of SSA: Operation Blackboard (OBB), Teacher Training, Free Text Books, Civil Works, Maintenance & Repair of Schools Buildings, School Grant, Teacher Grant, Training of Community Leaders, Education of Children with Special Needs (CWSN), Management & MIS Management Structure - (a) District Level Implementation Authority and (b) District Project Implementation Unit (DPIU), Education for Girls, Education of SC and ST Children, Computer Education, and Early Childhood Care Education (ECCE).

4. Rationale of the Study:

Now a day there is a general feeling that the teachers do not have satisfaction in their jobs. There seems to be growing discontentment on the part of the teachers towards their job as a result of which standards of education are falling. It is a fact that the teachers are really dissatisfied inspire of the different plans and programme which have been implemented to improve their lot.

The successful running of any educational system depends mainly upon the teachers, the pupil, the curriculum and the facilities. Of these, the teacher is the most important one and is the pivot on whom the entire educational structure rests. In order to strengthen the educational system it is indispensable to bring quality in primary education. First because a strong and healthy primary education can help in building the entire educational ladder up to the fullest perfection. Therefore much importance is too given to the elementary level. In this context the national policy of education (1986) in its programme of action (1992) has envisaged a strong knowledge based, work oriented primary education system through appropriate curricular, sufficient infrastructure provision of women teachers, supply of the teaching materials, through a scheme called operational black board.

Teachers with dedication, devotion and commitment are hence required to run the institution. Therefore, requirement of teachers at the elementary level has been given the topmost priority. In the present juncture teachers even with higher qualification prefer to work in elementary school. But the question remain whether they are satisfied with job of teaching in the elementary school eludes everybody. Naturally the following question are raised-

Are they the experienced or the in experienced teachers?

Are they the regular teachers or the Para teachers?

Are they the male teachers or the female teachers?

Are they the teachers of urban area or rural area?

For the answers of these questions the investigator has selected this research problem.

5. Objectives of the Study:

The study was conducted with the following objectives:

To estimate the level of job satisfaction of teachers at the elementary level both regular teachers and Para teachers.

To compare the level of job satisfaction of the regular teacher and Para teachers, male and female teachers, experienced and inexperienced teachers, rural and urban teachers at the elementary level.

6. Hypotheses of the Study:

The following hypotheses were formulated in connection with the objectives stated:

Ho_1 The elementary school teachers are not satisfied with their job.

Ho_2 There is no significant difference in the level of job satisfaction of regular and Para teachers.

Ho_3 There is no significant difference in the level of job satisfaction of male and female teachers.

Ho_4 There is no significant difference in the level of job satisfaction of experienced and inexperienced teachers.

Ho_5 There is no significant difference in the level of job satisfaction of rural and urban teachers.

7. Operational Definitions of the term used:

Job satisfaction here refers to favorable and unfavorable telling with which employees view their work in an affective and emotional response in regards to job requirement demands and expectations of the employees. This word refers to Dixit (1998) and job satisfaction scale. According to Dixit (1998) Job satisfaction, is the feeling of joy and pleasure that a person has at the work he is engaged in what does he feel about the work he does, decides it is linked with his set of mind. It seems to his personal concern.

This is not all. This could also be linked with the monetary rewards or the wages that he gets. As a whole all that is there at his work place determines job satisfaction. What inspires him, gives him a sort of thrill to be at his best at the job us a source of his job satisfaction. What keeps him out of place at the job, works against the job satisfaction that he could have. Job satisfaction serves him as his motivation to do the work.

Elementary level here refers to the teachers are working at the class I to VIII, lower primary and upper primary. Some teachers are regular and some teachers are para teachers.

Para teachers here refer to those who are working temporary or contractual under SSA project.

Experienced teachers here refer to those teachers who have 5 years and above 5 years teaching experience.

Inexperienced teacher here refers to those teachers who have below 5 years teaching experience.

8.   Delimitation of the Study:

The study has been delimited to 50 regular and 50 para teachers of Siliguri in Darjeeling educational district of West Bengal only. Other consideration could not be taken due to paucity of time. Because most of the schools in the Siliguri city in Darjeeling district. West Bengal are the three levels that are elementary (lower and upper primary), secondary & higher secondary and tertiary whether the elementary teachers are satisfied in their job when they view secondary and tertiary level of teachers in and around themselves. The study was conducted on that view point. The sample was categorized as per the intra-variables stated earlier after random selection.

CHAPTER TWO

REVIEW OF RELATED LITERATURE

A review of related literature is a vital component of the research process. Many studies on job satisfaction of teachers have been conducted abroad and in India. A research project is always a relief against a background of past studies in the same field. A survey of related literature enables the investigator to see that the study has been largely supported by a number of other studies and it is settled on a firm ground. The research studies reviewed in this chapter include closely related investigations carried out in India and abroad. The review of studies in the area of job satisfaction of teachers' studies has been conducted. The researches done in India as well as abroad in the related area are chronologically presented to gain an insight into the nature of the researches undertaken over the years.

2.1.Studies Conducted in India:

Chopra (1986) found that the teachers working in schools with open climate are likely to show higher overall job satisfaction than their counterparts in closed climate school. Further, in open climate, school teachers exhibit higher job satisfaction in respect of two areas, namely supervision and identification with the institution. The study reveals that school climate is an essential condition for job satisfaction among teachers.

Srivstava (1986) examined the extent of job satisfaction among primary school teachers and to make suggestions for creating a suitable environment in primary education. He found out that primary teachers were found to have high job satisfaction, female teachers compared to male, unmarried teachers as compared to married teachers, urban teachers as compared to rural teachers and non-agricultural family occupational background teachers were significantly higher in job satisfaction.

Agarwal (1998) on a sample of female teachers of primary schools conducted that more effective teachers had problems of job satisfaction due to social factors.

Reddy and Reddy(2000) in a study observed that the teachers employed under private managements were the most satisfied while those in the government managements were the least satisfied.

Gupta (2001) made an attempt to study satisfaction at three levels of teaching that is primary, secondary and college level. The investigator found that primary school teachers were more significantly less satisfied with their jobs. But the teachers at the Secondary and Tertiary levels express high satisfaction in their jobs.

Dixit (2002) conducted a study to measure job satisfaction among primary and secondary school teachers. The effect of sex, teaching experience and medium of instruction on the level of satisfaction with their profession were the predicting variables of the study. The investigator found different levels of satisfaction among primary and secondary school teachers being affected by sex, teaching experience and medium of instruction.

Vyas (2002) studied the job satisfaction of primary school teachers with reference to sex, marital status and educational qualification; found that sex was not related to job satisfaction f primary school teachers in Porbandar and Junagad districts of Gujrat. Married teach ere more positive towards job satisfaction than unmarried teachers of primary schools. Educational qualification was not related to job satisfaction of primary school teachers.

Reddy and Reddy (2003) in his study found that over qualified primary teachers had lo job satisfaction while teachers younger in age had higher level of job satisfaction, which had positive correlation with attitude towards teaching and job involvement.

Abbasi (2003) conducted a comparative study of job satisfaction among primary school teachers in Iran and India. It was revealed that in both countries, Iran and India, (a) More than 50% of teaches have medium level of job satisfaction, which shows that both countries have serious problems about situation of teachers in their societies and educational system, (b) In both countries, teachers have more satisfaction about social status aspect of their job. (c) In both countries, teachers have less satisfaction about economic sufficiency aspect of their job. (d) Female teachers in both countries have more economic sufficiency and interpersonal cooperation than male teachers, (e) Male and female teachers in this study do not have the same level of job satisfaction and gender was a factor, which affects their job satisfaction. (f) There is no significant difference between teachers with varied groups of age and their job satisfaction.

Lahiri and Saxena (2003) studied relationship of personality and personal factors with job satisfaction of primary school teachers. He found that there is a significant relation between job satisfaction and Introversion-Extroversion. A significant difference was found on job satisfaction of trained and untrained teachers. However, there was no significant difference on job satisfaction found in relation to marital status and degrees obtained by primary school teachers.

Agarwal (2004) in a study of job satisfaction of primary and secondary school teachers conducted that caste, place of work and mother tongue were significantly related to job satisfaction. Male graduate trained teachers, single family teachers, more experienced and government school teachers were more satisfied than other; age and marital status however had no relationship with job satisfaction.

Raj and Mary (2004) attempted a study on Pondicherry region and fond that job satisfaction was not high. Overall job satisfaction level showed that 39 percent of the Government school teachers had low (40% had average and 21% high) level of job satisfaction. No significant difference was fond in job satisfaction between gender, medium of instruction, place of work, educational qualification, salary and religion. There was no significant difference among teachers irrespective of experience, age, subjects and type of schools.

Rawat (2004) found out that level of job expectation played a significant role in determining job realities of teachers as also the job satisfaction which had positive relation with humanistic creative, social and aesthetic values and negative correlation with political and economic values.

Kumar (2005) found that the teachers with less job satisfaction are more prone to perceived stress than those with average or high job satisfaction and a teacher with favourable personality characteristics experiences, less stress than those with less favourable personality characteristics.

Bindu and Sudheesh Kumar (2006) studied the job satisfaction and stress coping skills of primary school teachers, and found that job satisfaction differentiated male and female primary school teachers and there is positive correlation between job satisfaction and stress coping skills.

Panda (2007) concluded a study to find out the level of job satisfaction of Para teachers in comparison with the primary teachers and observed that the Para teachers were highly dissatisfied.

Basu (2009) studied job satisfaction and mental heath among teachers: A survey. He found that job satisfaction does have a significant relationship with mental health in case of primary school teachers. When gender, marital status and locality of the primary school teachers were taken into consideration, satisfied teachers evinced significantly better mental health than their unsatisfied counterparts.

Shukla (2009) studied teaching competency, professional commitment and job satisfaction of primary school teachers. He found that there is high positive correlation between commitment to profession and job satisfaction level of primary school teachers. This meant that teachers who are satisfied with their job are also equally committed to their profession. There was very low positive correlation between teaching competency and job satisfaction. This meant that job satisfaction level do not affect competency skills of the teachers. There is very low positive correlation between professional commitment and teaching competency. This meant that professional commitment and teaching competency are not related to each other which meant that teachers are committed need not be competent and vice versa. There was no significant difference between teaching competencies level of teachers with high and average levels of job satisfaction. Teachers with different levels of job satisfaction did not showed any difference in level of their competency skills.

Ghosh (2013) the studied on "Job satisfaction of teachers working at the primary school". The findings of the study reveled that para, female, govt. school and under graduate teachers are more satisfied on their job than the regular, male, pvt. schools and graduate teachers.

Khurana (2013) studied Organizational Climate and Job Satisfaction of Teachers in Schools. School climate refers to the nature of situation and interaction that prevails between the teachers and head of the institutions. The study is conducted with an objective to investigate the types of organizational climate that exist in the higher secondary schools and its overall influence on the job satisfaction of Postgraduate teachers working in such schools The nature of the study is Normative Survey. Organizational Climate Descriptive Questionnaire and the job satisfaction scale were administered to the 100 teachers working in senior secondary schools of District Panchkula. The analysis revealed a significant difference in the school organizational climate and the job satisfaction of teachers. Job satisfaction was same among the teachers irrespective of their Marital Status, location of school, type of school they work except their sex. However, it is interesting to note that the open type of climate leads to very high level of job satisfaction among the teachers.

Sahoo and Sahoo (2014) studied the Job satisfaction of Teacher educators in relation to their perception of organizational climate. The study was conducted with the objectives like to study the level of job satisfaction of teacher educators, to study the pattern of organizational climate of B.Ed. colleges as perceived by the teachers, to study the relationship of perception of organizational climate and job satisfaction of the Teacher educators and to compare the male and female teachers perception on job satisfaction and organizational climate. It was conducted on a sample of 55 teachers (Male – 19 and Female – 36) of 10 Government B.Ed. colleges of Odisha. The findings of the study are, no significant difference exist in the level of job satisfaction of male and female teachers, the organizational climate of the B.Ed. colleges has no significant relationship with job satisfaction of teachers, the perception of male teachers regarding the organizational climate has no significant relationship with their job satisfaction and the perception of female teachers regarding the organizational climate has no significant relationship with job satisfaction.

Rani and Rani (2014) conducted a study on the influence of organization climate of elementary schools on job satisfaction of elementary teachers. The sample was drawn of 100 elementary school teachers by using Random Sampling Technique from Rohtak District, Haryana. The findings of the study showed that organizational climate of elementary schools is negligibly correlated with job satisfaction. This correlation shows that the job satisfaction of elementary teachers is not affected by organizational climate. The study also reveals that there is no correlation between the organizational climate of elementary schools and job satisfaction of female teachers.

2.2. Studies Conducted Aboard:

Davis (1977) conducted a study to locate various sources of satisfaction of teachers in their job. It was observed that the primary sources of satisfaction of teachers were in aspects of working with students, intellectual stimulation, autonomy, holidays and job security.

Birmingham (2001) conducted a study to find out gender difference in job satisfaction and that women teachers were more satisfied with their job than men teachers. The teachers were most satisfied with intrinsic reinforces such as social service, creativity, variety and ability utilization.

Michaelown (2002) conducted a study on teacher's job satisfaction, student's achievement and cost of primary education in Francophone and made an attempt to study what were the factors determining teacher's job satisfaction and how does teachers job satisfaction translate into learning outcomes and which cost efficient measure could be suggested in order to increase teachers job satisfaction.

Sergeant (2005) conducted a study on job satisfaction of primary teachers in Rural North-west China and fond out the impact of community factors school environment and teacher's characteristics had great impact on the job satisfaction of the teacher. Major findings of the study are: 1) Primary teachers are more satisfied in community with great economic and social; research and in communities that are less remote. 2) Primary teachers are more satisfied with better economic resources in schools. In schools where the work load is lighter and in schools, where there is organizational climate characterized by experienced leadership that support teachers collaborations. 3) Young teachers, male teachers, unmarried teachers and teachers with greater human capital were less satisfied.

Jasmim (2006) conducted a study on job satisfaction among primary teachers in Bangladesh and examined how male and female primary teachers perceive the term job satisfaction and what factors cause them to be satisfied or dissatisfied and found out of that female teachers consider primary teaching as a noble profession. They sketch the job as getting honour and social status. And male teacher's job satisfaction is to get a permanent job.

Bunnell (2008) found out that major improvement is needed in the incentives for primary teachers working in rural schools, such as providing rural allowances and good quality having and the teacher's wages need to be increased.

Adenike (2011) conducted a study on Organisational Climate as a predictor of Employee Job Satisfaction: Evidence from Convenant University. The study aim to explore organizational climate as a predictor of employee job satisfaction of academic staff from a private Nigerian University. The study of the antecedents of job satisfaction is important because of the role it plays in job satisfaction of employees which in turn affects organizational productivity. Data were collected from three hundred and eighty-four academic staff of the university with the aid of questionnaire out of which a total of two hundred and ninety-three questionnaires were returned fully and appropriately filled. Three hypotheses were tested and the results of the finding showed a significant positive relationship between these two variables. Thus, the study then paves way into other research opportunities in the field to stretch the depth of knowledge into public universities- i.e. the federal and state universities. It also serves as eye opener to conduct the research into other zones in Nigeria to see whether their organizational climate in relation to job satisfaction of the academics in those places will differ from what we have in the south-west Nigeria. Therefore, apart from confirming a theoretical proposition, the findings of this study are likely to have significant practical value.

Sabri, Ilyas and Amjad (2011) studied on Organisational culture and its impact on the Job Satisfaction of the University Teachers of Lahore. Education standard in developing countries like Pakistan is considered to be very low than education standard in developed countries. Lack of existence of supportive organizational culture in education sector may be one of the important reasons of this. Supportive organizational culture may raise the level of job satisfaction of teachers and satisfied teachers may produce healthy, satisfied and creative minds. Present study aims to determine the effect of organizational culture on job satisfaction level of teachers of public and private sector higher education institutes and universities of Lahore which is second largest city of Pakistan and a hub of higher education. Data were collected from a sample of 347 teachers through structured questionnaire. Principal Component Analysis was employed to test the construct validity. Regression analysis was conducted to determine the effect of organizational culture on job satisfaction of teachers. Empirical findings show that organizational culture is categorized into two components i.e. organizational culture related to managers and leaders (OCM) and organizational culture related to employees (OCE). In this study effect of both kinds of culture on job satisfaction is positive and significant. However, we observe that effect of OCE on job satisfaction is higher than effect of OCM.

Sharma, S., Hamid, J. and Rahim, N.M. (2013) studied on the relationship between organizational climates with job satisfaction of educational teachers at high school grade of Ardabil city. This study has been carried out as correlation-descriptive and scale based type research. The statistical community of the recent study is including the whole high school teachers of Ardabil City; the numbers of these teachers were 82 people based on the statistics and information of education office that the sampling was carried out by total-counting method. Two questionnaires of Liel Susman and Sam Deep (1989) organizational climate questionnaire (OCQ) and Visoki and Crome (1994) job satisfaction questionnaire were applied to collect the related data in this regard. The raw data using SPSS 18, descriptive statistics (distribution tables, percents, mean and deviation) and inferential statistics accordance with smirnov kolmograph test result based on data normality and Pearson correlation was used in this case. The results represent the fact that there is a positive significant correlation between the organizational climate and job satisfaction. (p =0.01, r =0.112). The results of correlation coefficient between the dimensions of organizational climate and job satisfaction showed that there is a significant relationship between the target agreement, role agreement and agreement on approaches of organizational climate dimensions with the job and job satisfaction. However, there was no found a significant relationship between the target, role agreements and satisfaction on the approaches of organizational climate dimensions with coworker, optimization and from job satisfaction point of view. There were no found significant relationships between the effectiveness of the relations from the organizational climate dimensions with the whole dimensions of job satisfaction and connection between the praise satisfaction with organizational climate with job, optimization and payment from the job satisfaction. There was observed a significant relationship between the satisfactions from praise with the peer.

2.3. Major findings of Reviews:

The major findings of the reviews revealed that,

There was difference in the level of job satisfaction due to gender variation, trained and untrained teachers.

Job satisfaction of elementary school teacher compared with Para-Teachers, the latter being highly dissatisfied.

Positive correlation existed between job satisfaction and stress coping skills.

Satisfied teachers had better mental health than the dissatisfied teachers.

From this the investigator got a clue to identify teachers who are satisfied and who are not satisfied.

CHAPTER THREE

METHODOLOGY

This chapter deals with the methodology of the present investigation. The method of study has been elaborated in detail right from the design, selection of sample, tool used, procedure followed for the collection of data and technique of data analysis and procedure. The statistical measures adopted for achieving the objectives and testing of hypotheses of this investigation has been placed in this chapter.

3.1.The Design of the Study:

The purpose of the study is to find out the level of job satisfaction in elementary school teachers in relation to gender, nature of job, teachers experience and locale. The study of design was a normative survey study. It is also a descriptive study of 'ex-post facto' type because of the fact that the job satisfaction of elementary school teachers have been studied as they feel in normal conditions and situations and evidences concerning the existing situation would be secured and norms would be identified to compare the present passions for further plan of action. The other methods like historical study designs were not adopted on the following of grounds.

Application of historical method of research was not thought to be appropriate for the study in the context of its objectives. This historical method of research is ideally suited for a study which is interested in analyzing a phenomena, event or conditions in the context of forces and factors which operated in the past. For this it makes use of external and internal evidences as well as of the primary services of information. It is needless to say that the present investigation does not aim at tracing the gradual development of teachers' job satisfaction. It confined its scope for studying the job satisfaction of elementary school teachers. For such a purpose survey study seemed to be more appropriate.

3.2.Population of the Study:

Approximately out of 25 elementary schools situated in and around Siliguri city, 10 schools were selected for study. Out of 500 teachers, 100 teachers were selected for study.

3.3. The Sample of the Study:

The samples of the study were drawn from 10 different elementary level schools of Siliguri city in Darjeeling educational district of West Bengal. In the present study a sample of 100 teachers was randomly selected of which 50 regular and 50 Para teachers, 50 male teachers and female teachers.

The sample for the study was drawn from the elementary schools of Siliguri city of Darjeeling district at West Bengal while selecting the sample case was taken to have a representative sample of nature of job, gender, teachers' experience and locale category. The teachers were categorized as regular and Para teachers, male and female teachers, below 5 years and above 5 years experienced teachers and rural and urban teachers. On the basis of the above mentioned studies, the sample had been categorized under these four types and it is presented in table 1.

Table 1: Details of the Sample

Variation	Group	Number
Nature of Teacher	Regular Teacher	50
	Para Teacher	50
Gender	Male	50
	Female	50
Teaching Experience	Below 5 years	55
	Above 5 years	45
Locale	Rural	50
	Urban	50
Total		100

3.4. The Tool Used:

In the present study investigator used the English version of Dixits job satisfaction scale (1998), developed by Panda (2007) for the process of data collection. The tool used essentially in the form of questionnaire having open choices. Detail description of the tool used had been given below.

The English version of Dixit's job satisfaction scale (1998), developed by Panda (2007) was adopted for the study. The scale consists of 50 items on 5 point scale and is Likert scale. The responses to be scored 5 to 1 for strongly agree, agree, undecided, disagree and strongly disagree respectively all are positive items, the validity and reliability of the scale are related to content validity and test retest reliability of 0.93 respectively.

There is no right or wrong answer for any item. It is self administrated scale. It could be given to a group of teachers at a time. They take 10-15 minutes to work on it. It is a true point scale .these are SA- strongly agree, A- agree, UD –undecided, D- disagree, and SD- strongly disagree. The teachers give responses to each of the 50 statements by in circling any one of the 5 alternatives.

The positive statement on the scale for their responses of SA, A, UD, D and SD were recorded as 5, 4, 3, 2, 1. The scoring order of 1, 2, 3, 4 and 5 was followed negative statements. The reliability of the scale was measured by test, retest method. The reliability coefficient in test –retest was found to be 0.93 respectively. The values represent the reliability measures of consistency and stability to a greater extent.

3.5.The Techniques of Data Analysis:

Techniques of data analysis for the present investigation included techniques for collection of data, scoring, interpretation of scores in relation to the objectives stated and hypotheses formulated.

Both descriptive and differential was adopted. For assessment of level of job satisfaction mean, median, mode and standard deviation was calculated for differentiating high, average and low level of job satisfaction which was expressed in terms of percentages. χ^2 and 't' ratio were calculated for finding out significant difference in job satisfaction of the contrasts.

3.6. The Procedures:

Selection of sample, Administration and scoring of the tools, Preparation of the data sheet, Data organization and analysis, Interpretation of the result, Preparing the report & references.

CHAPTER FOUR

ANALYSIS AND INTERPRETATION

4.1. Organization of Data:

The present chapter focuses on the collection of data and the results emerging there from on the objectives of the present study is to assess the level of job satisfaction of elementary school teachers. Teachers job satisfaction scale developed by Dixit (1998), developed by Panda (2007) was used to measure the job satisfaction of the teachers. The details of it had been presented in previous chapter. The results had been presented fewer than two major sections. The first sections include administration and scoring of the task. In the second section the results had been presented by both the descriptive and inferential statistics.

4.1.1. Administration of the Tool:

The administration procedure for the tool was followed by some norms and conditions. The investigator had a take personal case in giving directions to the teachers for answering questions. The head masters of the schools were required to extend their cooperation of a successful conduct of the study. The job satisfaction scale of Dixit (1998) developed by Panda (2007) was administrated. The selected teacher's were 100 over the questionnaire requesting them to give their responses at their leisure hour.

4.1.2. Scoring of the answer sheet:

All the 50 items were scored as for the instructions given in the manual of the test. In manual each statement have responses, like strongly agree (SA), agree (A), undecided (UD), disagree (DA), strongly disagree (SDA) are scores 5, 4, 3, 2 and 1. All the responses are indicating teacher's job satisfaction. From the scores of teachers is respective percentile we are found. From this percentile, level of satisfaction was decided.

4.1.3. Organization of data on job satisfaction of teachers working at the elementary level:

After the administration of the job satisfaction scale, the answer sheet was scored and compiled class interval were made and presented in table 2.

Table 2: Frequency distribution of the total sample and sub samples on job satisfaction of teachers working at the elementary level.

Scores	Frequencies								Total
Variation	Nature of job		Gender		Teaching Experience		Locale		
Sub sample	Regular	Para teacher	Male	Female	Below 5 years	Above 5 years	Rural	Urban	
211-220	1	8	2	7	5	4	2	7	9
201-210	11	12	9	14	12	11	12	11	23
191-200	15	16	17	14	14	17	23	8	31
181-190	16	3	11	8	7	12	8	11	19
171-180	5	7	6	6	8	4	7	5	12
161-170	1	3	3	1	3	1	3	1	4
151-160	1	1	2	0	1	1	0	2	2
TOTAL	50	50	50	50	50	50	55	45	100
	100		100		100		100		

After the completion of the scores on job satisfaction, it was observed that the scores on job satisfaction of teachers working at the elementary level ranged from 151-220. From the distribution presented in table 2, It was observed that maximum scores clustered in the class interval of 191-200. Therefore, the class interval 191-200 was considered to be the model class interval. On scrutiny of the table it was revealed that the same trend was also observed in case of Nature of job, Gender, Teachers experiences and locale variation. The frequency polygon drawn on the total sample had been shown with the smooth frequency curve being super imposed on it in figure (i). Then the cumulative frequency curve in terms of ogives were drawn and presented in figures (ii), (iii), (iv) and (v) in respect of nature of job, gender, experience and locale variation.

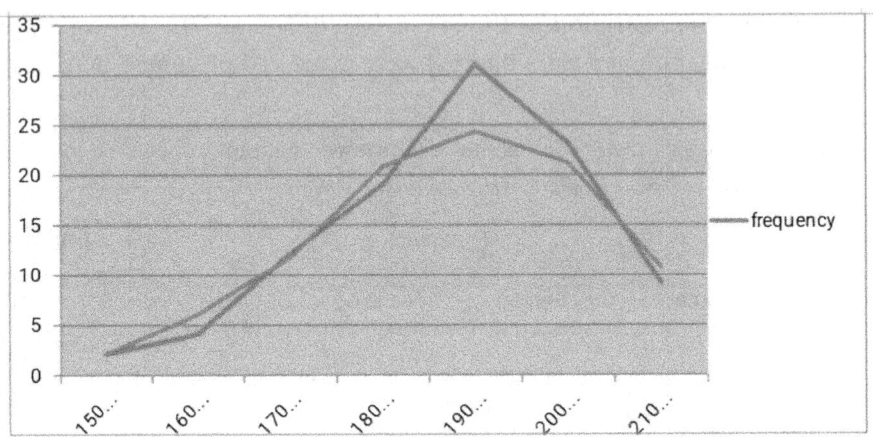

Figure (i) Frequency polygon of the scores on job satisfaction with Smoothed frequency curve super imposed of teachers working at the elementary level.

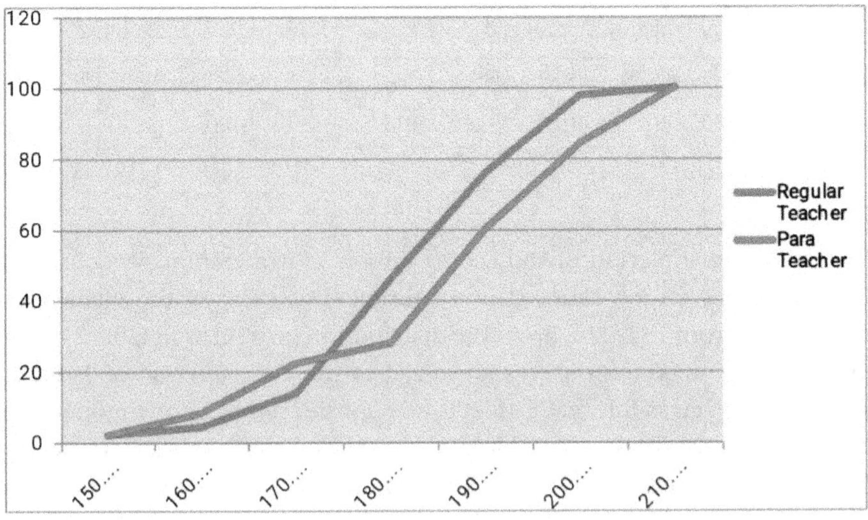

Figure (ii) Cumulative Frequency of Regular and Para Teacher's on the scores of job satisfaction of teachers working at the elementary level.

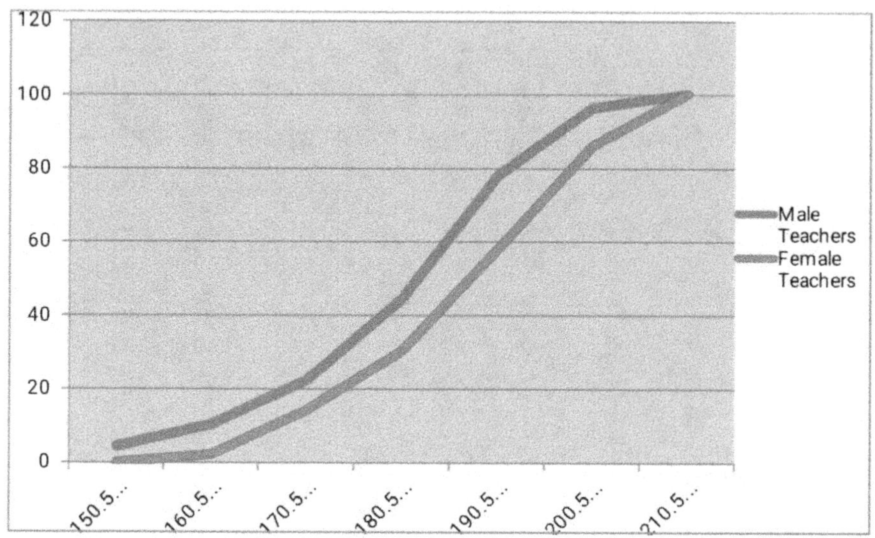

Figure (iii) Cumulative Frequency of Male and Female teachers on the scores of job satisfaction of teachers working at the elementary level.

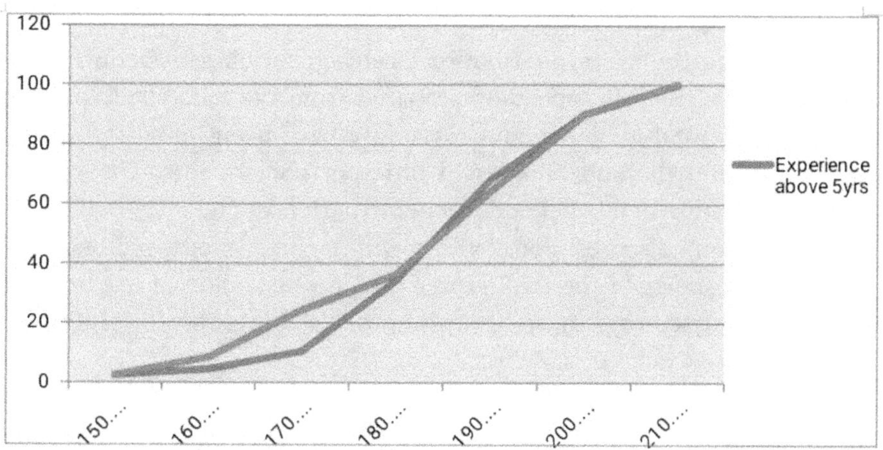

Figure (iv) Cumulative Frequency of Experience Below 5 years and Above 5 years on the scores of job satisfaction of teachers working at the elementary level.

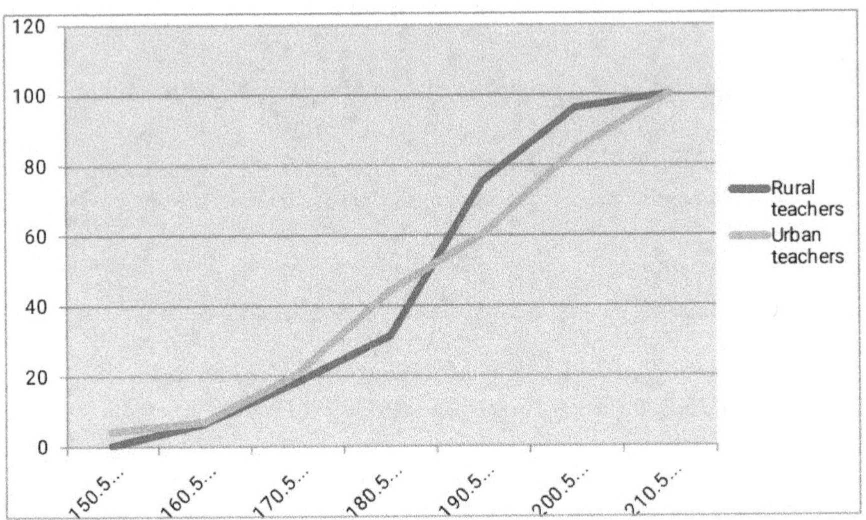

Figure (v) Cumulative frequency of Rural and Urban teachers on the scores of job satisfaction of teachers working at the elementary level.

4.1.4. Descriptive Measures on Job Satisfaction of Elementary School Teachers:

For studying the score distribution on teachers job satisfaction scale, a frequency distribution table was prepared from the data sheet and the measures of central tendency and variability have been found out of the total sample and the sub samples in different components. The sample consisted of Nature of job, gender, teacher experiences and locale variation. The distribution of scores along with mean, median, mode and standard deviation in respects of the total scores on job satisfaction of teacher and sub sample wise scores has also been computed and presented in table 3.

Table 3: Measures of Central Tendency and Standard Deviation of Sub Samples and Total Scores on job satisfaction of elementary school teachers

Variation	Group	Numbers	Mean	Median	Mode	SD
Nature of job	Regular Teacher	50	191.5	190.9	189.7	11.7
	Para teacher	50	195.1	197.38	201.94	15.4
Gender	Male Teachers	50	190.1	192.26	196.58	13.9
	Female Teachers	50	196.5	197.64	199.92	12.85
Teaching experience	Below 5 years	50	193.1	192.16	189.8	14.9
	Above 5 years	50	194.7	195.20	196.2	12.6
Locale	Rural	55	193	194.86	198.58	11.9
	Urban	45	193.5	194.07	195.21	15.8
Total		100	193.30	194.7	198.3	13.7

The above table reveals that the mean, median, mode and standard deviation on job satisfaction of elementary school teachers differed in the 4 variables like Nature of job, gender, teaching experience and Locale. When sub sample wise mean score were analyzed it was found that the Para teachers, Female teachers, experienced teachers (above 5 years) were satisfied in their job compared to their counterpart.

From the total score of the job satisfaction of teachers it was found that the mean, median, mode being 193.3, 194.7, and 198.3 respectively did not coincide having slight deviation. Hence, the total distribution of scores tends to be deviated slightly from normality. The scale has four variables like Nature of job, Gender, Teacher experience and Locale.

The mean scores in the total sample and different sub samples were presented in bar graphs figure (vi) to have a clear view of their job satisfaction of teachers working at the elementary level.

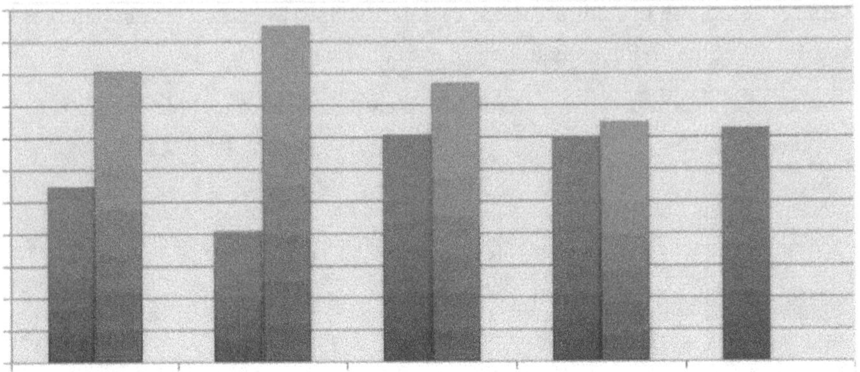

Figure (vi) Bar diagram showing the mean scores of the sub samples along with the total sample on job satisfaction of elementary school teachers.

4.1.5. Categorization of the sample according to the differential level on job satisfaction of teachers working at the elementary level:

To find out the percentage of teachers in different degree of their job satisfaction, the total sample was categorized under 3 categories like teachers having high, average, and low of job satisfaction. This was done according to the percentile values of P75, P25. The scores ranging less than P25, P25 to P75 and above P75 were considered as low, average and high job satisfaction. The number and percentage of the teachers in their differential levels of job satisfaction presented in table 4.

Table 4: Categorization of the sample in their differential level on job satisfaction of teachers working at the elementary level:

Categories	Score Range	No. of sample	% of sample
High	204 and above	24	24%
Average	184 to 203	54	54%
Low	183 and Below	22	22%

It was revealed from the above table that the percentage of teachers on high, average and low levels of their job satisfaction was 24%, 54% and 22% as against 16%, 68% and 16% respectively. Hence it can be concluded that the teachers in their differential level of their job satisfaction were not normally distribute.

The percentage (%) of the teachers according to the differential levels of their job satisfaction of teachers working at the elementary level was shown in figure (vii).

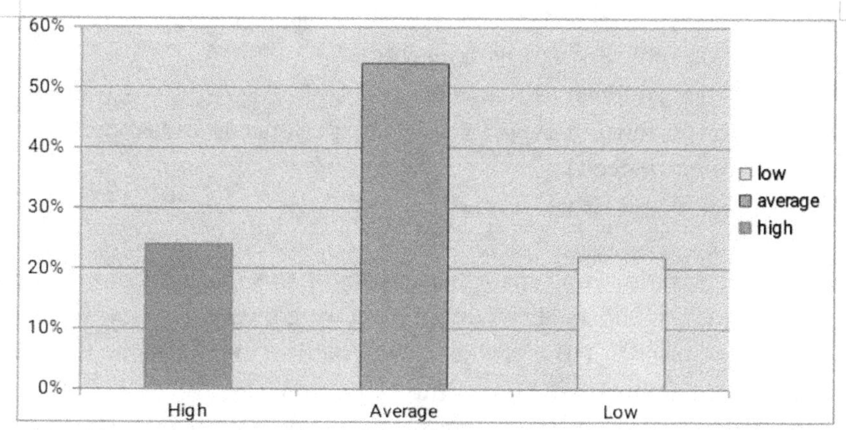

Figure (vii) Categorization of the sample according to differential levels of job satisfaction of teachers working at the elementary level.

4.2. Statistical Analysis and Interpretation:

The chapter was dealt with an introduction based on the background data in the context of the problem. This had a strong rationale with a special reference to the review of literature. The methodology and procedure constituted the second chapter, where in a detailed description of the design, tools used, technique of analyses and procedure were presented. In the present chapter, attempts have been made to statistically analysis the data and test the hypotheses by rejecting or accepting them as would be the cases.

The study was mainly a normative type of study where attempts have been made to find out the job satisfaction of teachers working at the elementary level. It envisaged the study level of job satisfaction of Regular and Para teacher, Male and Female teacher Experienced (above 5 years) and Inexperienced (below 5 years) teachers and Rural and Urban teachers. In this section, attempts have been made to verifying the data in accordance with the objectives and hypotheses formulated. All the data were analysis as per the assumption of parametric data for job satisfaction.

The sample was further grouped as sub sample on the bases of nature of job, gender, teaching experience and locale for job satisfaction in elementary school teachers. Analysis of this sample was done to verify the null hypothesis which has been determined earlier. Thus the samples were split into the following sub-samples.

- Nature of job - Regular and Para teachers.
- Gender - Male and Female teachers.
- Teacher's experience- Below 5 years (inexperienced) and Above 5 years teachers (experienced).
- Locale – Rural and Urban teachers.

This categorization was made basing upon the socio- economic and cultural situation of the locality sample from were drawn.

4.2.1. Assessment of the teachers on equal distribution in their job satisfaction of teachers working at the elementary level:

One of the objectives of the study was to categorize the elementary school teachers in differential level of their job satisfaction. For this hypotheses formulated was 'the elementary school teachers are not equally satisfied with their job'. In order to test the hypotheses the χ^2 test of equality was calculated and found to be 19.29. The χ^2 to be significant at 2 degree of freedom at 0.05 level is 5.99 and at 0.01 levels is 9.21. The calculated value was significant at 0.01 levels. Hence the null hypotheses 'the elementary school teachers are not equally satisfied with their job' was rejected, and it can be concluded that the elementary school teachers were equally distributed in their differential levels of job satisfaction.

4.2.2.Sub sample wise differential analysis on job satisfaction of teachers working at the elementary level:

The present sub sample has been attempt to meet the objective of testing the null hypotheses (Ho) stated earlier and presented in the report in earlier chapter. In case of each sub samples, first the null hypotheses have been set up according to the requirements of the problem. The level of significance for the test has been selected and they were subjected to the test significance on the basis of 't' value for corresponding degrees of freedom. The calculated value of 't' was compared where a decision rule was framed. If the calculated value of 't' is uses then the table value of 't' the null hypothesis was accepted and interpretation of results was made accordingly.

4.2.2.1. Nature of job wise differential analysis on job satisfaction of teachers working at the elementary level:

In the present study, Nature of job was taken as an intra-variable and the sample was divided in two categories. They were Regular and Para teachers. The test of not significance of difference between the mean scores of Regular and Para teachers on their job satisfaction of teachers working at the elementary level was calculated and result were shown in the table 5.

Table 5: Summary of the test of significance of differences between the mean score of Regular and Para teachers on job satisfaction of elementary school

Variation	Sub sample	No	Mean	SD	SE_D	't'	Remarks
Nature of job	Regular	50	191.5	11.7	2.73	1.32	Non Significant
	Para teacher	50	195.1	15.4			

Critical value of "t" with df 98 at 0.01 = 2.63 and at 0.05 = 1.98

On perusal of the above table, it was found that 't' ratio (1.32) was not significant as the 't' ratio (1.32) was less than the table value of 't' at 0.05 level (1.98) an at 0.01 level (2.63) at 98 degree of freedom. Therefore the null hypothesis that "there is no significant difference in the level of job satisfaction of Regular and Para teacher" could not be rejected. It thus indicates that nature of job did not have significant impact on the job satisfaction of teachers working at the elementary level. The Para teachers were found to be more satisfied in their job satisfaction than their counter parts. This was in conformity with earlier researches of Shukla (2009) and Panda (2007).

4.2.2.2. Gender wise differential analysis on job satisfaction of teachers working at elementary level:

In the present study, Gender was taken as an intra-variable and the sample was divided in two categories. They were Male and Female teachers. The test of not significance of difference between the mean scores of male and female teachers on their job satisfaction of teachers working at the elementary level was calculated and result were shown in the table 6.

Table 6: Summary of the test of significance of differences between the mean score of Male and Female teachers on job satisfaction of elementary school

Variation	Sub sample	No	Mean	SD	SE$_D$	't'	Remarks
Gender	Male	50	190.1	13.9	2.68	2.39	p < 0.05
	Female	50	196.5	12.85			

Critical value of 't' with df 98 at 0.01 = 2.63 and at 0.05 = 1.98

On perusal of the above table, it was found that 't' ratio (2.39) was significant as the 't' ratio (2.39) was less than the table value of 't' at 0.05 levels (1.98). But the 't' ratio (2.39) is more than the table value of 't' at 0.01 levels (2.63) at 98 degrees of freedom. Therefore the null hypothesis that "there is no significant difference in the level of job satisfaction of male and female teachers" was rejected. It thus indicated that the male and female teachers did not differ significantly in their job satisfaction working at the elementary level. The female teachers were found to have more job satisfaction than their counter parts. The female teachers think it is the most suitable job for them, where as the male teachers do not rate teaching as a profession. The female teacher feels satisfaction in teaching profession only because they think the profession suitable for them. This study was conformity with the research conducted by Abbasi (2003) and Ghosh (2013).

4.2.2.3. Teachers Experience wise differential analysis on job satisfaction of teachers working at elementary level:

In the present study, Teachers Experience was taken as an intra-variable and the sample was divided in two categories. They were Below 5 years (inexperienced) and Above 5 year's (experienced) teachers. The test of not significance of difference between the mean scores of Below 5 years and Above 5 years teachers on their job satisfaction of teachers working at the elementary level was calculated and result were shown in the table 7.

Table 7: Summary of the test of significance of differences between the mean score of Below 5 years and Above 5 years teachers on job satisfaction at elementary school

Variation	Sub sample	No	Mean	SD	SE$_D$	't'	Remarks
Teachers Experiences	Below 5 yrs	50	193.1	14.9	2.76	0.58	Non Significant
	Above 5 yrs	50	194.7	12.6			

Critical value of 't' with df 98 at 0.01 = 2.63 and at 0.05 = 1.98

On perusal of the above table, it was found that 't' ratio (0.58) was not significant as the 't' ratio (0.58) was more than the table value of 't' at 0.05 level (1.98) an at 0.01 level (2.63) at 98 degree of freedom. Therefore the null hypothesis that "there is no significant difference in the level of job satisfaction of below 5 years and above 5 years teachers" could not be rejected. It thus indicated that experience did not have significant impact on the job satisfaction of teachers working at the elementary level. The teachers belonging to more Above 5 teachers were found to have more favorable job satisfaction than their counter parts. This was in conformity with earlier study of Abbasi (2003).

4.2.2.4. Locale wise differential analysis on job satisfaction of teachers working at elementary level:

In the present study, Locale was taken as an intra-variable and the sample was divided in two categories. They were Rural and Urban teachers. The test of not significance of difference between the mean scores of Rural and Urban teachers on their job satisfaction of teachers working at the elementary level was calculated and results were shown in the table 8.

Table 8: Summary of the test of significance of differences between the mean score of Rural and Urban teachers on job satisfaction at elementary school

Variation	Sub sample	No.	Mean	SD	SE$_D$	't'	Remarks
Locale	Rural	55	193	11.9	2.84	0.17	Non Significant
	Urban	45	193.5	15.8			

Critical value of 't' with df 98 at 0.01 = 2.63 and at 0.05 = 1.98

On perusal of the above table, it was found that 't' ratio (0.17) was not significant as the 't' ratio (0.17) was less than the table value of 't' at 0.05 level (1.98) an at 0.01 level (2.63) at 98 degree of freedom. Therefore the null hypothesis that "there is no significant difference in the level of job satisfaction of Rural and Urban teachers" accepted. It thus indicates that don't have significant impact on the job satisfaction of teachers working at the elementary level. The teachers belonging to more urban teachers were found to have more favorable job satisfaction than their counter parts. This was in conformity with earlier researches of Ghosh (2013).

CHAPTER FIVE

SUMMARY AND RECOMMENDATION

5.1. The Summary:

Teachers have always played vital roles in the reconstruction of the society. In the event of universalisation of elementary education, therefore much emphasis was placed on recruitment of teachers. Teachers are accorded great due to their manipulative skills in igniting the inherent talents of the children. Hence NCTE (1998) put emphasis on teacher education as only enlightened and emancipated teachers can lead communities and nations in there march towards better and higher quality of life. Recent thrust on elementary education is intended to increase enrolment, retention and reduce drop and rates by achieving success through SSA/DPEP programs. Hence the following activities were given due importance.

- Operation Blackboard scheme.
- Strengthening of teacher education in content and pedagogy.
- Nutritional support for all children.
- Making the school an attractive place.
- Innovative and alternative education.
- Inclusive Education.

In all these activities, teacher improvement was the only solution. Hence capacity building of teachers thought to be the priority area at the primary level. Therefore a community based SSA was launched. Under SSA intervention, immediate recruitment of Para teachers was made who were directed to work as elementary school teachers. They were given in service training and hints to look into the quality dimensions of education with a paltry salary not commensurate with their educational qualifications. But whether teachers working at those levels are satisfied or not, this was where looked. Hence the target of reaching at the aim of universalisation of elementary education is skill at stake. This has been quite pertinent from the reviews cited here under. The successful running of any educational system depends mainly upon the teacher, the pupil, the curriculum, and the facilities. Of these, the teacher is the most important one and is the pivot on whom the entire educational structure rests. Teacher was regarded as a holy person in ancient India; he was compared to a God. He is to be treated as a combination of the Trinity (Brahma, Vishu, Maheswara) as well as the supreme one. Thus, teacher was regarded as the most perfect being in those days and teaching was considered as a holy duty. As per our Indian ancestors, the "Teacher" is God. Further, it is said, 'Guru Brahma, Guru Vishnu, Gurudeva Maheswara' which implies that the teacher is the creator, the sustainer and the ultimate liberator. Centuries ago, in this Indian Land of Vedas, certain principles which had something noble and uplifting about them were held steadfastly. These principles were emphasized in those famous verses in Sanskrit, which the teacher and the taught recited together an considered the essence of their mutual relationship: "Saha Naavavatoo / Saha Naubhuraktu / Saha Viryam Karavahai / Tejarvi Naava Dhitamastu / Mavidvisavahai": May he protect us both; May he save us both; May we do together great deeds; May our bearing be bright; May we have each other: Though the same lines are recited today, one does not always find the same zeal and the same enthusiasm. The teacher's image has unquestionably changed from an 'inner-directed' to that of a 'stereotype'.

Teaching is a very complex activity and multidimensional in nature besides knowledge in theory, it demands on the part of the teachers a variety of skills and abilities to be displayed. As the skills and efficiency of the teacher largely influence the pupils learning, recruitment of efficient and skilled teacher into the educational system becomes an essential pre-requisite of improvement of the system. Therefore, it becomes primarily an obligation of education to obtain capable and efficient teachers as learning by pupils depends very much on upon the skill and potentiality of the teacher, how we exploits the potentialities of his pupils to acquire knowledge and skill. It has also been stressed in the National Policy of Education, 1986. In this connection in the Program of Action it has been categorically mentioned that there should be sincere attempt for a substantial improvement in the quality of teacher's education. Teacher's accountability to the pupils, their parents, and community and to their own profession is a matter of grave concern in the present context. Hence, the importance of good teaching staff in the process of education is the only criterion to step in the progress of developing countries.

Rationale of the Study:

The successful running of any educational system depends mainly upon the teachers, the pupil, the curriculum and the facilities. Of these, the teacher is the most important one and is the pivot on whom the entire educational structure rests. In order to strengthen the educational system it is indispensable to bring quality in primary education. First because a strong and healthy primary education can help in building the entire educational ladder up to the fullest perfection. Therefore much importance is to given to the primary level. In this context the national policy of education (1986) in its programme of action (1992) has envisaged a strong knowledge based, work oriented primary education system through appropriate curricular, sufficient infrastructure provision of women teachers, supply of the teaching materials, through a scheme called operational black board.

Teachers with dedication, devotion and commitment are hence required to run the institution. Therefore, requirement of teachers at the elementary level has been given the topmost priority. In the present juncture teachers even with higher qualification prefer to work in elementary school. But the question remain whether they are satisfied with job of teaching in the elementary school eludes everybody. Naturally the following question are raised-

- Are they the experienced or the in experienced teachers?
- Are they the regular teachers or the Para teachers?
- Are they the male teachers or the female teachers?
- Are they the teachers of urban area or rural area?

Answers to the above questions let the researcher to conduct the present study on job satisfaction.

Objectives of the Study:

The study was conducted with the following objectives:

To estimate the level of job satisfaction of teachers at the elementary level both regular teachers and Para teachers.

To compare the level of job satisfaction of the regular teacher and Para teachers, male and female teachers, experienced and inexperienced teachers, rural and urban teachers at the elementary level.

Hypotheses of the Study:

The following hypotheses were formulated in connection with the objectives stated:

HO_1 - The elementary school teachers are not satisfied with their job.

HO_2 - There is no significant difference in the level of job satisfaction of regular and Para teachers.

HO_3 - There is no significant difference in the level of job satisfaction of male and female teachers.

HO_4 - There is no significant difference in the level of job satisfaction of experienced and inexperienced teachers.

HO_5 - There is no significant difference in the level of job satisfaction of rural and urban teachers.

Operational Definitions of the term used:

Job satisfaction here refers to favorable and unfavorable telling with which employees view their work in an affective and emotional response in regards to job requirement demands and expectations of the employees. This word refers to Dixit (1998) and job satisfaction scale. According to Dixit (1998) Job satisfaction, is the feeling of joy and pleasure that a person has at the work he is engaged in what does he feel about the work he does, decides it is linked with his set of mind. It seems to his personal concern. This is not all. This could also be linked with the monetary rewards or the wages that he gets. As a whole all that is there at his work place determines job satisfaction. What inspires him, gives him a sort of thrill to be at his best at the job us a source of his job satisfaction. What keeps him out of place at the job, works against the job satisfaction that he could have. Job satisfaction serves him as his motivation to do the work.

Elementary level here refers to the teachers are working at the class I to VIII, lower primary and upper primary. Some teachers are regular and some teachers are para teachers.

Para teachers here refer to those who are working temporary or contractual under SSA project.

Experienced teachers here refer to those teachers who have 5 years and above 5 years teaching experience.

Inexperienced teacher here refers to those teachers has below 5 years teaching experience.

Scope and Delimitation of the Study:

The study has been delimited to 50 Regular and 50 Para teachers of Siliguri city in Darjeeling educational district, West Bengal only. Other consideration could not be taken due to pan city of time.

The Design:

The purpose of the study is to find out the level of job satisfaction in elementary school teachers in relation to gender, nature of job, teachers experience and locale. The study of design was a normative survey study. It is also a descriptive study of 'ex-post facto' type because of the fact that the job satisfaction of elementary school teachers have been studied as they feel in normal conditions and situations and evidences concerning the existing situation would be secured and norms would be identified to compare the present passions for further plan of action.

Population of the Study:

Approximately out of 25 elementary schools situated in and around Siliguri city, 10 schools were selected for study. Out of 500 teachers, 100 teachers were selected for study.

The Sample:

In the present study a sample of 100 teachers was randomly selected of which 50 regular and 50 para- teachers. The sample for the study was drawn from the elementary schools of Siliguri city in Darjeeling district at West Bengal while selecting the sample case was taken to have a representative sample of nature of job, gender, teachers' experience and locale category.

The Tool used:

In the present study investigator used the English version of Dixits job satisfaction scale (1998), developed by Panda (2007) for the process of data collection. The tool used essentially in the form of questionnaire having open choices.

The Techniques of data analysis:

Techniques of data analysis for the present investigation included techniques for collection of data, scoring, interpretation of scores in relation to the objectives stated and hypotheses formulated. Both descriptive and differential was adopted. For assessment of level of job satisfaction mean, median, mode and standard deviation was calculated for differentiating high, average and low level of job satisfaction which was expressed in terms of percentages. χ^2 and 't' ratio were calculated for finding out significant difference in job satisfaction of the contrasts.

5.2. The Major Findings:

The study gave the following findings –

i. The elementary school teachers were not equally distributed in their job satisfaction.

ii. There existed no significant difference in the level of job satisfaction of regular a para teacher's variation. However, from the mean scores it was revealed that the para teachers were more satisfied in their job than the regular teachers.

iii. There existed significant difference in the level of job satisfaction of male and female teacher's variation. However, from the mean scores it was revealed that the female teachers were more satisfied in their job than the male teachers.

iv. There existed significant difference in the level of job satisfaction of below 5 years and above 5 years experienced teacher's variation. However, from the mean scores it was revealed that the above 5 years experienced teachers were more satisfied in their job than the below 5 years experienced teachers.

v. There existed significant difference in the level of job satisfaction of rural and urban teacher's variation. However, from the mean scores it was revealed that the rural and urban teachers were equally satisfied in their job.

5.3. Recommendations:

The study of the present investigation reveals that the person, who is in charge of selecting the teaching personal in our country, should be informed about the very composite criteria of job satisfaction.

The present selection procedure for recruitment of teachers for schools is dove mostly on the basis of post academic record. It does not consider the candidates traits and aspects which can make him component in the field of teaching. This result in selection of teachers probably, in most of the cases misfit for the profession. Such profession misfits of the teaching profession further accelerate the deterioration of the system as a whole. As much depends upon the efficiency of the teachers, the progress of nation hampers due to ill equipped teachers. Hence, it becomes a prime to attract more and more qualified and intelligent students towards teaching profession so we have to make this profession more attractive by provide different facilities so that they will be more interested to serve as a teacher with a greater degree of job satisfaction.

In this concertino some of the recommendations given by UNESCO may be stated:

i. There should be close co-operation between component authorities, organization of teachers, of employers and workers and of parents as well as cultural organization and intuitions of learning and research, for the purpose of defining educational policy and precise objectives.

ii. Authorities should establish and regularly use recognized means of consultation with teachers' organizations on educational policy and school organization, upon new developments in the education service and upon the effects of administrative requirements on the word of teachers.

iii. Teacher's organizations should be entitled to participate in making policy and in developing standards relating to teaching and to enter into the profession.

iv. Better promotional venues and incentives may be provided at all levels to all the teachers without any prejudice.

v. Teachers need proper rest room and other physical facilities, up to-date teaching equipments and instructional materialism the schools in which they serve.

vi. Salary of the school teachers need to be increased keeping in view the rise in price index.

5.4. Suggestions for Further Research:

In the length of the present research and its results, it is suggested to undertake he studies in a methodical way and with wider approach in order to bring into focus the variables and areas which were not incorporated in this study. The present study was conducted on 100 teachers in elementary school.

i. Studies can be replicated on large sample by including whole or more districts so as to present better picture of the studies made.

ii. The present study can be made on a large and more representative samples, which would help us, provide more reliable result.

iii. Studies may be taken up to study the job satisfaction of teachers working in secondary, higher secondary schools and colleges.

iv. Studies may be taken up to identify the psychological factors that contribute for job satisfaction.

v. Studies may be taken up on experimental basis to enhance the job satisfaction of teachers.

Bibliography

Alyaha & Mbogo (2017). Demographic Factors Affecting Teachers' Job Satisfaction and Performance in Private Primary Schools in Yei Town, South Sudan. IRA International Journal of Education and Multidisciplinary Studies (ISSN 2455-2526), 8(1), 142-148. doi: http://dx.doi.org/10.21013/jems.v8.n1.p14

Belfield, C., & Heywood, J. (2008). Performance pay for teachers: Determinants and consequences. Economics of Education Review, 27, 243-252.

Bender, K. A., & Heywood, J. S. (2006). Job satisfaction of the highly educated: The role of gender, academic tenure, and earnings. Scottish Journal of Political Economy, 53(2), 253- 279.

Bogler, R. (2001). The influence of leadership style on teacher job satisfaction. Educational Administration Quarterly, 37(5), 662-683.

Bashir, L.(2019). Job Satisfaction of Teachers in Relation to Professional Commitment. International Journal of Indian Psychology, 4, (4). 52-59.

Chamundeswari, S. and Vasanthi, S. (2009). Job Satisfaction and Occupational Commitment among Teachers. Edutracks, 8(6), 29-31.

D.Jan & Jeo. A (2020) "Professional commitment and job satisfaction among secondary school teachers." Educational Quest-An International Journal of Education and Applied Social Sciences

Eichinger, J. (2000). Job Stress and Satisfaction among Special Education Teachers: Effects of Gender and Social Role Orientation, International Journal of Disability, Development and Education, 47(4), 397-412.

Fatima, K. (2002). Job Satisfaction Among Secondary School Teacher – An Investigation. An Unpublished Doctoral Thesis, Jamia Milia Islamia University.

George, E., Louw, D and Badenhorst, G (2008). Job Satisfaction among Urban Secondary School Teachers in Namibia, South African Journal of Education, 28(1), 135-154.

Ghazi, S. R.and Maringe, F. (2011), Age, Gender and Job Satisfaction among Elementary School Head Teachers in Pakistan, Education, Knowledge & Economy: A Journal for Education and Social Enterprise, 5(1-2), 17-27

Hansuman, W.& Goiring (2001). Rethinking the profession of teaching: A progressive option. *Action inTeacher Education, 12*(1), 1-5.

Johnson, S. M., Kraft, M. A., & Papay, J. P. (2012). How context matters in high-need schools: The effects of teachers' working conditions on their professional satisfaction and their students' achievement. *Teachers College Record*, 114(10), 1–39.

Kataria, S. (2014). Job Satisfaction among Government and Private School Teachers, Educational Confab, 3(6), 6-11.

Kitchel, T., Smith, A., Henry, A., Robinson, J. S., Lawver, R., Park, T., & Schell, A. (2012). Teacher job satisfaction and burnout viewed through social comparisons. Journal of Agricultural Education, 53(1), 31-44.

Koustelios, A.D. (2001). Personal Characteristics and Job Satisfaction of Greek Teachers, International Journal of Educational Management, 15(7), 354 – 358.

Khetal, A. (2011). A Study of the relationship between Teacher Effectiveness and Job Satisfaction of teachers in teaching in higher secondary schools. In Abstracts of Educational Research in India, The M.S. University of Baroda, Vadodara: CASE.

Lavingia, K.U. (1974). A Study of Job Satisfaction Among School Teachers. In NCERT. (ed.) (1972-76). Second Survey of Research in Education (p 438). New Delhi: NCERT.

Lata and Sharma (2017). Teacher commitment and teachers' self-concept as predictors of job satisfaction.

Liu, X., & Ramsey, J. (2008). Teachers job satisfaction: Analysis of the teacher follow-up survey in the united states for 2000-2001. Teacher and Teacher Education, 24, 1173-1184.

Menon, M. E. and Athanasoula-Reppa, A. (2011). Job Satisfaction among Secondary School Teachers: The Role of Gender and Experience, School Leadership and Management, 31(5), 435-450.

Okpara, J. O., Squillace, M. & Erondu, E. A. (2005). Gender differences and job satisfaction: a study of university teachers in the United States. Women in Management Review, 20(3), 177-190

Rao, M.N and Samiullah S (2016). Job Satisfaction and Mental Health among School Teachers, International Journal of Humanities and Social Science Research, 2(8), 23-29.

Sood and Anand. (2010). *Attitude towards teaching profession and job satisfaction of teachers. Edutracks9, 8, 36-38.*

Tasnim, S. (2006). Job Satisfaction among Female Teachers: A Study on Primary Schools in Bangladesh, M.Phil. Dissertation, University of Norway.

Tyree, L. (1996). Commitment Profiles: combination of organizational commitment and job satisfaction. Journal of Vocational behaviour, 67 (03) 270 -280.

Appendix

JOB SATISFACTION OF TEACHERS WORKING AT THE PRIMARY LEVEL UNDER SSA INTERVENTIONS

This is the job satisfaction scale for the study of satisfaction you have when you are teaching the children of classes. This is meant for the teachers who teach students of class I to VIII in primary schools. The job satisfaction of teachers was liked with 6. Factors as their: 1. Nature of job. 2. Gender 3.Teachers experience 4.Educational qualification 5. Locale and the 6.Managment of primary schools. These 6 factors had been expressed in 50 statements. Please read each statements carefully, encircle one of the five alternatives given in the answer sheet.

Each statement has 5 responses. Like strongly Agree (SA), Agree (A) Undecided (U), Disagree (DA), and strongly Disagree (SDA).All the responses are correct and indicate your job satisfaction. Select the response whatever would be felt most suitable for you. Respond all statements. What is wanted to you do it as fast as you can. You may take 15 to 20 minutes.

Job Satisfaction of Teachers Working at the Primary Level under SSA Interventions

STATEMENTS:

1. You are fit for the teaching job in nature and character.
2. Your institution is at the right place in regards to its function.
3. Your salary is according to your nature of work.
4. Your institution is education oriented.
5. You are feeling that your head of the institution is fit for the post.
6. All your teachers are working with the spirit of co-operation among themselves.
7. The students appreciate you.
8. Your position in the society is respectable for adopting this profession.
9. Your profession is enabling you to educate your children and ward.
10. Your institution is very need and cleans where anybody would desire to work.
11. You feel exhilarated in your teaching job.
12. There is scope of promotion in your profession.
13. You are getting scope to reader advice in the planning of your institution.
14. The head of your institution is impartial.

15. The curriculum transaction programme in your school is progressing nicely.
16. You are feeling ease at working with your colleagues and feeling happy with them.
17. Your relatives and friends are respecting your profession.
18. You are getting opportunity to look after your family.
19. There is provision of getting extra financial aid in doing extra work.
20. The time table of your institution is appropriate to you.
21. The head of your institution and yourself show interest to work for others.
22. Your students are appreciating you as a teacher.
23. You feel comfortable to accommodate yourself with your salary.
24. There is proper arrangement of light and air in the classrooms.
25. You feel pleasure during holidays.
26. You are independent in your work.
27. You appreciate the behavior of your head and others.
28. You feel that there is proper rapport in your school between the teachers and the taught.
29. Your laboratory is adequately equipped.
30. You appreciate to switch over to any other profession in this scale of pay after retirement.
31. You feel that you are secured until you are working.
32. You get praise from your senior colleagues for your work.
33. You get scope to develop rapport with the guardians of your students.
34. The student-teacher ratio in your school is helping you not to work more.
35. You feel that future of teaching job is bright.
36. You are getting books from your library for your use.
37. Your colleagues are interested to help you at the time of need.
38. Your institution is an example for others in respect of administration.
39. You are able to help your children in building the carrier and character of your students.
40. You are getting scope to partake in games and sports in addition to your teaching job.
41. Your colleagues see you in par with them.
42. Your classroom is well decorated as per necessity
43. You feel that not to be transferred from your institution is a matter of joy.

44. You are getting scope to enhance your professional competency.
45. You are getting scope to participate in other co-curricular activities in addition to games and sports.
46. Audio-visual aids are available in your school.
47. You do not feel any problem to reach in your institution.
48. You feel that seating accommodation available in the class is more than sufficient in comparison with the student strength.
49. You feel pride in your profession.
50. You get scope after retirement.